Elemental Things

Poems by
Michael S. Glaser

Second Place Winner of The Poetry Box Chapbook Prize, 2022

Poems ©2023 Michael S. Glaser
All rights reserved.

Editing & Book Design: Shawn Aveningo Sanders
Cover Design: Robert R. Sanders
Author Photo: Mia Schmidt

No part of this book may be republished without permission
from the author, except in the case of brief quotations
embodied in critical essays, epigraphs, reviews and articles,
or marketing collateral.

Second Place Winner of The Poetry Box Chapbook Prize, 2022
ISBN: 978-1-956285-28-4
Printed in the United States of America.
Wholesale Distribution via Ingram.

Published by The Poetry Box®, February 2023
Portland, Oregon
ThePoetryBox.com

for Kathleen—
who has gifted me with her love, kindness, and wisdom

Contents

The Presence of Trees	7
Snake	8
Rebekah	9
The Fourth Day	10
Solitude	11
Vagaries	12
Stillness	13
Late April Thoughts	14
Elemental Things	16
Noise	17
Letter to My Fifth Grade Teacher	18
The Grandchild of Love	20
Morning Walk	21
O!	22
Studies of Dawn	24
In the Men's Room	26
Cheekbones	27
Cancer	28
Brief Bio	29
May Day, Betpouey, the Pyrenees	30
The Woods	31
Acknowledgments	33
Praise for *Elemental Things*	35
About the Author	37
The Poetry Box® Chapbook Prize	39

The Presence of Trees

Slowly, I am remembering
the language of awe,

how to take in, say,
the living complexity of a tree

its gnarled trunk,
its ragged bark,

the way its leafy canopy
filters sunlight

down to the brown
carpeted ground,

the way the wind bends my heart
to the exquisite presence of trees

the forest that calls to me as deeply
as I breathe,

as though the woods were
marrow of my bone as though

I myself were tree, a breathing, reaching
arc of the larger canopy

beside a brook bubbling to foam
like the one

deep in these woods,
that calls

that whispers *home.*

Snake

Back in the days of our childhood,
before complexity reared its reptilian head,

back when life was a carousel
with both reason and rhyme,

back before the paradox of reality
began to reveal itself—

we stood in the arms of innocence
imagining the bliss of our first parents,

their happy garden state.

Rebekah

~for Katie Coogan-Raley

*This is the story of Isaac, son of Abraham.
Isaac was forty years old when he took to wife Rebekah,
The daughter of Bethuel the Aramean...*
—Genesis 25:19

Perhaps it is not so much
that we are loved,
as that we can love,

perhaps that is the secret...
to love even our own pain
and, after all that time,

to make something from it

so that it too might blossom,
might illumine the circles
in which we are called to dance.

Imagine Isaac, after the ram,
learning to love all over again.

The Fourth Day

…and on the fourth day,
without access to the internet,
a certain lightness of being
began to penetrate,

a sense of freedom
so startling
I thought perhaps
I had freed myself
from an addiction

and was able, at last,
to hear the sound
of my own heart
singing.

Solitude

In solitude, at ease with myself
and able to return to my spirit
when it has been shaken
bearing witness to the world,

I can reclaim my vulnerability
and not have to compromise
with the demons that pull at my soul.

In solitude, I embrace that liminal junction
where what has been and what will be
are joined with the wisdom of my ancestors

who remind me
that I do not have to wrestle
with God to be blessed.

Vagaries

How do I honor the mysteries
that lace my life

Like the freshness of the air
after lightening,

the Spring green of leaves
before they ripen

or the labyrinth of paths that have led me
to this exact place and this exact moment?

* * *

Might I learn to celebrate
what I can't understand?

How, for example, the bee turns pollen into honey,
how cicadas re-emerge after their long sleep,

how the Milky Way contains more suns
than earth can imagine

or how all the vagaries of life
led us, one to the other

soft eyes to soft eyes,
in a smile that suddenly whispered

YES!

Stillness

The stillness is beautiful.
can one say that?
Beautiful stillness?

Or the *quiet of insects?*
To say, "I don't know"
is not poetic. Or is it?

What can a poem know better
than its own not knowing?

* * *

Thirty-three thousand feet up, an airplane
is travelling from somewhere to somewhere else.
Like us, travelling through time and stillness,

through space and busyness from wherever
to wherever, which, perhaps, is why
stillness is so beautiful. Like the quiet of insects.

Like not knowing.
Like simply being,
right here, right now.

Late April Thoughts

I

What the Gun Knows about Fear—

That it is more powerful than a bullet,
burrowing deeply—
delighting in its darkness.

The gun knows how randomly
it can burst upon us
frighten us, claim us.

II

What the Sun Knows about Violence—

That the world is large
that each spring the earth blooms again.

The sun knows that somewhere
it is always dark,

and somewhere
there is always light.

III

What the River Knows about Love—

That it flows through laughter and tears
that it has its own song.

The river knows its waters
will endure.

The river knows
to trust where it flows.

Elemental Things

The world today is sick to its thin blood
for elemental things.
—Henry Beston

Riding the freeway, what we know
is the feel of cowhide, the future
framed in a window that looks out at a sea
of concrete and dangerous machines.

We move from here to there and back again,
commute long distances, listen to the news,
music, talk radio. We become impatient,
angry, do foolish things

curse our fellow travelers going 80
like us back and forth,
back and forth
week after week after week.

If someone were to knock on our door
and invite us into elemental things –
earth, air, fire before the hands

water welling from the earth—
what would we answer?
How would we know to respond?

Noise

The unexamined life has always been in style.
Only recently has it become mandatory for enlightened people.
—Robert J. McShea

And I'm thinking about noise and distractions and satellites and cell phones and i-pods and wireless networks and microwaves cris-crossing the universe and flat screen HD TVs and pundits and politicians and wires in the ears of half the people I pass, and surround sound and surround I-MAX and iPads, and App after App after App and lap tops and the screech of the subway, the honking of traffic, and MP3 audio players in our automobiles so that sound can go on and on and on with hardly a hesitation, so that the silence we fear need never really enter here, so that whatever thoughts might sneak in need not be endured, so that no errant path will take us somewhere surprising and unexpected, or remind us of that quiet

wherein we might hear something
perilous and sacred
whispering.

Letter to My Fifth Grade Teacher

Dear Miss Lorenz:

I'm writing because I was remembering you today,
how soft and kind your voice was and how your eyes
sparkled with laughter and light

which is why I wanted to impress you
and why I was so afraid of spelling
where I knew you would discover
that I was just another stupid kid.

And so, on the day of the Big Spelling Test,
I made that tiny piece of paper
and when we put our books away,
I cupped it in my hand for use
only when absolutely necessary.

And you moved up and down
the rows of our desks
pronouncing words until
you stopped next to me,
called out a word and,
when everyone was writing,
reached into my clenched fist,
took the paper and then
walked on.

You never made an example of me,
never spoke to my parents about it,
or even mentioned it to me.
And you never treated me differently either,
just went on as though nothing had happened.

But, of course, something did:

I never cheated again, Miss Lorenz.
I never stole another candy bar
or money from the box
on the top of my father's dresser –
or from my mother's purse.

And I am writing to thank you
for treating me with dignity
even as you caught me,
red-handed in sin.

It was as close to Grace as I have ever been.
Perhaps someday I'll know it once again.

The Grandchild of Love

Look deeply into her eyes.
See the old soul there,
simple and wise.

She asks for little:
some attention, a book to read,
pictures to point at, someone to listen.

She is embraced by joy.
She embraces joy.

Nurture this.
Nurture *this*.

The rest
you'd best not meddle with.

Morning Walk

I

Returning from her morning walk,
she glows as she tells me

how the sun foretold its arrival
turning the sky mauve and pink

before cresting orange and then,
as though giving birth to itself,

rose crimson out of the ocean—
spread its light onto the horizon,

and lifted up until it cleared the plane of the water
and cast its bright glow onto the crest of each wave.

Her words sparkle like ocean jewels.

II

While she was gone, I slept
and dreamt a rough scattering of morning dreams,

vestiges of yesterday playing out their anxieties
until I rose, clumsily, and remembered how

before she left, I felt the invitation of her touch
on my shoulder.

O

~in memoriam for Lisa Zsebedics
1965–1984

I

All these years later, reading a poem, and I find myself
remembering the conversation we had that Friday when
you told me you wanted to change your major, change your life.

On Sunday I woke to find you had been killed the night before,
riding on the back of your boyfriend's motorcycle,
hit by a driver who was drunk.

All day I thought about the bright threads you had discovered,
how they animated your eyes, your hands, your voice
as you embraced the poetry that invited your heart to dance.

Monday was breezy and sunny, as though
all your generous exuberance was outside now.
Inside, I read Auden's *Musée des Beaux Arts* to our class.

II

On Tuesday, unsure what to do with my grief,
I went to the memorial service, thinking your parents
would be there, thinking I might say something . . .

and I watched our silver-haired president follow your parents
into the commons, his head cocked to the right, as was his wont,
one hand in his pocket, one hand out.

At commencement the first scholarship in your name,
for a student majoring in what had been your major,
went to someone who was not you.

For years your parents returned to bestow the award
their grief palpable, handing an envelope
to this or that student who was not you.

III

Trapped as I was in my own curious grief,
I watched your parents in theirs.
Worlds separated us.

I did not know how what I knew could
fit into the healing that was trying to weave
its impossible way around their lives.

I still don't know.

Eventually only your brother came, and now the envelope
is handed out by the Provost, calling out many names
that few remember – tokens, prizes, a line on a résumé.

IV

I live with this poem that was you, Lisa Zsebedics,
a rough fragment,
an astonishing first draft.

I have become a keeper of its memory,
guardian of a light
still flickering in this world

wanting voice,
wanting, I imagine,
to exclaim

    O!

in all its mystery,
in all its silent awe.

Studies of Dawn

*Ruskin urged his students to think of their drawing exercises
as both a scientific record and as an act of worship
which had nothing to do with picture making.*
—sign on an exhibit

I

And Ruskin too, every day, painted the sacred shape –
the grace of a gladiola or the subtle Rose of Demeter,
its pulse mingling emerald and ruby as it played in the light.

II

Amazing, this language of the heart,
these brushstrokes in which the edge
of a boar's hair bristle

bends the stem of a paper narcissus
into the head of a heron
or a flat, broad sweep leaves behind

a dogwood petal
looking like nothing so much
as the ancient beard of God.

III

I hold these images faithfully,
try to understand the delicate caress
of such worship,

how hand and brush and color discover
the florescent flash, celebrate the ineffable
on blue-gray paper,

the awe of this sunrise or that storm,
the blessing of a long-stemmed iris,
the delicate jointing of an olive branch.

How brilliantly the colors body forth,
as though they spoke in the multi-lingual
tongue of the Holy Ghost,

breathing black to blue to orange to white:
a paradise itself, bathed and borne anew
in this subtle and shining light.

In the Men's Room

~for Michael Ellis-Tolaydo

> *oh pray that what we want*
> *is worth this running,*
> *pray that what we're running*
> *toward*
> *is what we want.*
> —Lucille Clifton

I am in the men's room and I hear him come in,
talking over his shoulder to a student about time

and I call out to say, "always teaching, aren't we?"
and I tell him about my son who called this morning
and the lovely thoughts we shared because
the electricity at his work was out.

And then he tells me about how he just called his wife
to tell her what a wonderful time he had Saturday,
simply being with her and talking

and I finish, and he finishes
and I read him a poem that I was reading
about time and about running,
and as we wash our hands
we agree that love is what matters

and then we hug,
right there in the men's room
before going back
to whatever it was we left
to find each other at this time
in this place for this
unimagined embrace.

Cheekbones

Slowly I am beginning to understand
why it is that tears appear
on the cheekbones of our elders

and why, in the midst of a conversation,
I have sometimes noticed a small pool
gathering.

I used to think it had to do with cold,
that age made eyes more vulnerable,
but yesterday, listening to my friend Tom

and seeing again those tears,
I think I began to understand
that eternal sadness we are born into

and the slow gathering of resignation
to the evidence that we have, indeed,
left the garden.

Mostly we like to imagine otherwise,
but in moments like yesterday
when words are spoken truly

we are reminded that life,
however beautiful, is temporal,
and what but tears can speak to that?

Cancer

On my way to work, the King Singers on the radio.
Their close harmonies soar—and I try to absorb
the sweetness of it,
to calm the errant growth, blooming inside.

On the cornfield to my left,
hundreds of migrating geese peck at the earth,
glean sustenance for their journey.
I envy their instinct, their innocence.

In a year how many of us will still be alive?

To my right the carcass of a deer
lies in the soybean field.
Plucked at by buzzards for almost a week,
its cavity is now exposed—

and I marvel at the logic of it all:
this giving of what remains to sustain the living
and the strange gratitude I feel
for this moment

with the King Singers, the migrating geese,
my cancer and the body of that deer—

the vibrant offerings of this singular, sunlit day.

Brief Bio

Old age has invited me
to embrace uncertainty

look in the mirror
of impermanence

and find there, at last,
my heart's true song

smiling and simply
humming to itself.

May Day, Betpouey, the Pyrenees

Last night a late Spring snow,
and today, sun and this hike
to the Shrine of St. Justin.

The mountain guides streamlets
of melting snow in a dance
that rushes past the blossoming spring flowers

so that everything seems fragile and fleeting
and flowing through the canyons
to the rivers and ocean below.

I like to believe that all things connect
like this, that each life and spirit, each
flower and stream connects, connects,

and that, if we are kind enough,
one to the other, we might know this,
hear it in the river's song, in the mountain breeze,

see it in the snow, in the colors of clouds
praising the sun as it rises
blessing the sun as it sets.

The Woods

The woods open me
to the mystery

of how patiently each tree
embraces the slow unfolding

of the seasons,
how unfailingly each seems to know

when to send forth buds
and when to let go.

I long for their certainty,
their trust in the resurrection of Spring.

Acknowledgments

The author wishes to express appreciation to the editors of the following books, journals, and websites in which the following poems first appeared, sometimes in earlier versions:

The Broadkill Review: "Morning Walk"

DanMurano.com: "Studies of Dawn" and "The Grandchild of Love"

Fledgling Rag: "May Day, Betpouey, the Pyrenees"

In Between Earth and Sky by Nalini M. Nadkarni (UC Press): "The Presence of Trees"

The Literary Review: "In the Men's Room"

Living Lessons (Whispering Angel Books): "Letter to My Fifth Grade Teacher"

Ocho: "Cheekbones"

The Patuxent Review: "Late April Thoughts"

The Raven's Perch: "Brief Bio"

Sacred Journey: "Rebekah"

The Threshold of Light (Bright Hill Press): "Studies of Dawn" and "Morning Walk"

Tree Magic (Sunshine Press): "The Presence of Trees"

The author also wishes to express his gratitude to the following whose guidance, nurture and close critical readings have helped to shape these poems:

Bill Palmer, Sara Eisenberg, Wayne Karlin, Daniel Sheff, Kathleen Glaser, Lucille Clifton, Father David Boileau and Tom Wisner.

Praise for *Elemental Things*

These poems return us to the sacred in our everyday lives, calling us back to "the language of awe," as the poet puts it so gorgeously in the opening poem. These poems feel both elemental and essential themselves, capturing so many holy moments in nature, inviting us into the solitude and presence from which absorbing poetry is born.

—James Crews, contest judge
poet, editor of *How to Love the World*

Elemental Things is filled with invitational pause reminding us that beneath the noise and pace we create, lies the overlooked blessings that have accompanied us all along. These are poems with room enough to allow the reader to incorporate their own experience and turn the small, uncertain, crumpled words inside our own fists into the kind of poem we want to live by. If pen to paper is a prayer—these are word temples.

— Deanna Nikaido, poet, educator, visual artist

I have long admired the wisdom and artistry of Michael S. Glaser's poems. He writes with compassion and depth, masterfully capturing the fragility, dignity, and complexity of the human condition. His poems remind us what a gift it is to be alive, even during difficult times. In *Elemental Things* he explores what it means to be blessed in a broken world and, like a modern-day Adam, he challenges us to awaken from the amnesia we experience when we forget to honor and connect with each other and the natural world. Every poem hints at ways we can move toward wholeness. Glaser's poems remind us, gently, to love who we are and what we can still become.

—Elizabeth Lund, reviewer and host of Poetic Lines

About the Author

Michael S. Glaser is a professor Emeritus at St. Mary's College of Maryland where he served for 50 years. A Poet Laureate of Maryland (2004–2009), Glaser has received awards for his poetry, his teaching, and his service to poetry and the poetic tradition in Maryland. A former Board member of the Maryland Humanities, and the Kirkridge Retreat and Study Center, he served as a Maryland State Arts Council Poet-in-the-Schools for nearly 25 years and now co-leads retreats which embrace the reading and writing of poetry as a means of self-reflection and personal growth.

Glaser has published several collections of his own poetry, edited three anthologies and co-edited *The Collected Poems of Lucille Clifton* (BOA 2012). He writes book reviews for *The Friends Journal* and is the proud father of five children and ten grandchildren. He now lives in Hillsborough, NC with his wife, the educator and Courage and Renewal facilitator, Kathleen W. Glaser.

www.michaelsglaser.com

The Poetry Box® Chapbook Prize

The Poetry Box® Chapbook Prize is open to both established poets and emerging talent alike. The contest is open to poets residing in the United States and is open for submissions each year during the month of February. Find more information at ThePoetryBox.com.

2022 Winners

Tracking the Fox by Rosalie Sanara Petrouske

Elemental Things by Michael S. Glaser

Listening in the Dark by Suzy Harris

2021 Winners

Erasures of My Coming Out (Letter) by Mary Warren Foulk

Of the Forest by Linda Ferguson

Let's Hear It for the Horses by Tricia Knoll

2020 Winners

The Day of My First Driving Lesson by Tiel Aisha Ansari

My Mother Never Died Before by Marcia B. Loughran

Off Coldwater Canyon by C.W. Emerson

2019 Winners

Moroccan Holiday by Lauren Tivey

Hello, Darling by Christine Higgins

Falling into the River by Debbie Hall

2018 Winners

Shrinking Bones by Judy K. Mosher

November Quilt by Penelope Scambly Schott

14: Antología del Sonoran by Christopher Bogart

Fireweed by Gudrun Bortman

www.ingramcontent.com/pod-product-compliance
Lightning Source LLC
LaVergne TN
LVHW090040080526
838202LV00046B/3901